Seeds of a Nation

Pennsylvania

Margaret Coull Phillips

KIDHAVEN
PRESS™

THOMSON
GALE

San Diego • Detroit • New York • San Francisco • Cleveland
New Haven, Conn. • Waterville, Maine • London • Munich

Picture Credits

Cover Photo: © Francis G. Mayer/CORBIS
© Bettmann/CORBIS, 15, 17, 25
© Burstein Collection/CORBIS, 12
© Corel Corporation, 10, 34, 38
© Kevin Fleming/CORBIS, 32
© Historical Picture Archive/CORBIS, 9, 18, 27
© Hulton/Archive by Getty Images, 8, 30, 35, 36
Chris Jouan, 5, 7
Library of Congress, 31, 33
© Francis G. Mayer/CORBIS, 23
© Franklin McMahon/CORBIS, 26
© Museum of the City of New York/CORBIS, 20

© 2003 by KidHaven Press. KidHaven Press is an imprint of The Gale Group, Inc., a division of Thomson Learning, Inc.

KidHaven™ and Thomson Learning™ are trademarks used herein under license.

For more information, contact
KidHaven Press
27500 Drake Rd.
Farmington Hills, MI 48331-3535
Or you can visit our Internet site at www.gale.com

LIBRARY OF CONGRESS CATALOGING-IN-PUBLICATION DATA

Phillips, Margaret Coull.
  Pennsylvania / by Margaret Coull Phillips.
    v. cm. — (Seeds of a nation)
Includes index.
Summary: Discusses the history of Pennsylvania, to include: Native
American tribes; early European explorers; colonization; founder
William Penn; and statehood.
  ISBN 0-7377-1023-3 (hardback: alk. paper)
  1. Pennsylvania—History—Juvenile literature. 2. Pennsylvania—Juvenile literature.
[1. Pennsylvania—History.] I. Title. II. Series.
  F149.3 .P486 2003
  974.8—dc21
                                                            2002009855

Contents

Welcome to Pennsylvania

Pennsylvania is unique in the history of the United States. As one of the original thirteen colonies, it was founded by William Penn in 1681, and it became a state on December 12, 1787. Pennsylvania was the second state to ratify the new U. S. Constitution.

Pennsylvania is close to the Atlantic Ocean, midway between New York State and the New England states to the north, and Maryland and the southern states to the south. It is the only one of the original thirteen colonies that has no land bordering the Atlantic coast.

Pennsylvania is nicknamed the "Keystone State" not only because of its geographical location, but also because of its place in the history of the United States. A keystone is the center stone that holds an arch together. As the United States was settled, the northern colonies became more industrialized, while the southern colonies depended more on farming or agriculture. Pennsylvania, because it was centrally located between the two regions, became the keystone that helped hold the colonies together. Many important conventions and meetings were held in its major city, Philadelphia. The Declaration of Independence was written and signed in Pennsylvania. The U. S. Constitution was written there as well. The First and Second Continental Congresses met in Philadelphia, and the city also served as the nation's capital during the Revolutionary War. Pennsylvania was the meeting place where the representatives of the thirteen colonies came together to begin the process of building a nation.

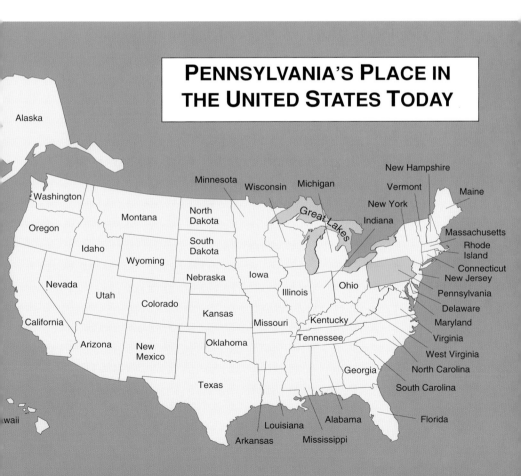

PENNSYLVANIA'S PLACE IN THE UNITED STATES TODAY

Chapter One

The Original Pennsylvanians

People lived on the land called Pennsylvania long before the European explorers, trappers, and settlers came. Thousands of years before Pennsylvania became a state, Native Americans made it their home. These Native Americans hunted for game in the thick forests, fished in the pure streams and rivers, and farmed their small fields. They had their own distinct cultures and languages. The original Pennsylvanians lived in groups called tribes. The names of some of these tribes were the Erie, the Monongahela, and the Shawnee. However, the largest and perhaps most important native tribes were the Lenni-Lenape and the Susquehannock. Scholars estimate that in the year 1600, about thirty thousand Native Americans lived in present-day Pennsylvania.

The Lenni-Lenape

The Lenni-Lenape (pronounced Len-nee Le-nah-pay) were an ancient tribe that was well respected among other Indian nations. A usually peaceful people, the Lenni-Lenape lived in small villages along what is now the Delaware River, which forms the eastern border of Pennsylvania. They lived in single-family houses made of bark and sapling poles. William Penn described the houses as being about as high as a grown man.

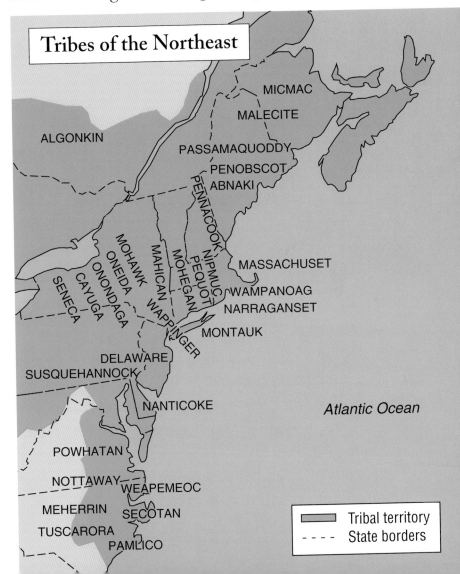

Tribes of the Northeast

MICMAC
MALECITE
ALGONKIN
PASSAMAQUODDY
PENOBSCOT
ABNAKI
PENNACOOK
NIPMUC
MASSACHUSET
MOHAWK
ONEIDA
MAHICAN
PEQUOT
MOHEGAN
WAMPANOAG
ONONDAGA
NARRAGANSET
CAYUGA
SENECA
WAPPINGER
MONTAUK
DELAWARE
SUSQUEHANNOCK
NANTICOKE
Atlantic Ocean
POWHATAN
NOTTAWAY
WEAPEMEOC
MEHERRIN
SECOTAN
TUSCARORA
PAMLICO

Tribal territory
- - - - State borders

Tishcohan (pictured) was a chief of the Lenni-Lenape tribe. The Lenni-Lenape were admired by many tribes of the Northeast.

The Lenni-Lenape society was **matriarchal**. That means that everything passed down through the mother's side of the family. The mother owned the home and fields. The children took their mother's name as their last name. In a divorce the mother kept the children. The Lenni-Lenape women were treated with great respect within their tribe or clan. The women were the farmers. They cultivated the land and grew food for the community. They grew what is called the "three sisters," corn, squash, and beans along with sweet potatoes and tobacco. They also harvested many types of wild berries and nuts.

The Lenni-Lenape were tall and strong. The men often shaved their heads with a sharp piece of flint, leaving just a crest of hair running down the center of their scalp. This hairstyle is also called a Mohawk. They greased this lock of hair so it would stand up, and they decorated it with shells. The women wore their hair long and placed shells and animal teeth in it. Both men and women painted their faces using a variety of colors. The women favored the color red and often painted it around their ears and eyes.

Men and women wore clothing made of skins, feathers, and plant fibers. The women wore dresses and the men wore shirts. Both wore deerskin leggings. Their clothing was decorated with shells, porcupine quills, and feathers. In the winter, fur robes replaced the lighter

The Lenni-Lenape women were greatly respected within their tribe.

Lenni-Lenape boys were taught to hunt and fish at an early age.

clothing worn in the summer months. The children dressed much the same as the adults except that in the hot summer, the very little children wore nothing at all.

The men hunted and fished. They hunted for deer, turkey, rabbits, and other game to supplement the vegetables grown in the fields. Hunting was also necessary in time of famine or if raiding tribes destroyed their food stores.

The Lenni-Lenape had no alphabet or written language. Their culture and history were passed down in the form of stories told to each generation. The children did not attend school; instead they were taught skills by their tribal elders. The boys were taught to hunt and fish. The girls were taught the art of dressing skins for clothing and household use, cooking meals, and cultivating fields.

For many years the tribe grew and thrived. It is estimated that in the year 1600, about twenty thousand Lenni-Lenape were living in the area of what is now eastern Pennsylvania.

The Susquehannock

Not as much is known about the Susquehannock Indians because they lived in the interior of Pennsylvania along the Susquehanna River. This river has several branches that flow through central Pennsylvania. These branches eventually flow together to form one river that finally empties into the Chesapeake Bay. Few explorers were able to get to the Susquehannock's villages and record their way of life. Most of the activity and exploration were done along the eastern edge of Pennsylvania. Captain John Smith did visit this tribe. In 1608, he left Virginia in search of **provisions** for Virginia Colony. When he sailed up the Susquehanna River close to what is now Pennsylvania, he was met

Susquehannock children help their mothers prepare a meal for the family.

by a group of Susquehannock. He wrote a detailed description of that meeting.

The Susquehannock lived in villages, and each village had a chief. They lived in longhouses, dwellings that were from sixty to eighty feet long. Several families occupied each house. The house had a door at each end and a hallway that ran down the center. In the hallway each family had a hearth for a fire with a hole above it to allow the smoke to escape. Bunks for sleeping were built along the walls. Each family's quarters were separated from one another by bark walls between the bunks.

The Susquehannock were farmers. Like the Lenni-Lenape, their society was also matriarchal. They, too, planted corn, squash, and beans. In the summer the tribe would often leave their villages and go south to the Chesapeake Bay to fish and collect shellfish. They would return each fall to harvest the crops, hunt for game, and prepare for the winter.

Unlike the Lenni-Lenape, the Susquehannock were fierce warriors. They raided the villages of the tribes close to the Chesapeake Bay. Along with being great warriors, the Susquehannock were also great traders. They were actively involved in the fur trade with the Swedes and the Dutch, who had set up forts along the Delaware River.

Before the first explorers came to Pennsylvania, scholars believe about seven thousand Susquehannock Indians lived in Pennsylvania. Once Native Americans had contact with Europeans, their lives changed forever. Most died from diseases brought by Europeans and from warfare with other tribes. By the Revolution in 1776, the once thriving native tribes were gone.

Chapter Two

The Europeans Arrive

In the late 1500s and early 1600s, many European countries such as France, England, and the Netherlands sent explorers to the New World. Like Spain, they were interested in finding a short way to the riches of the East Indies. Many explorers believed that a waterway through this new land would lead them to the Orient. This waterway became known as the Northwest Passage. To **finance** the explorers, a number of European trading companies were formed. One of these companies was the Dutch East India Company. Even though its main objective was to find a quick way to the Orient, it played an important role in the development of the new lands Columbus had found.

The Explorers

In August 1609, Henry Hudson, an Englishman exploring for the Dutch East India Company, entered the Delaware Bay and sailed all the way up to the mouth of the Delaware River. He called this river the South River. He did not come ashore because he realized that it was a dead end and not the Northwest Passage. He sailed out into the Atlantic the next day. He went on to discover the Hudson River, which was named after him. Hudson never did discover the Northwest Passage, but his backers in Europe were very impressed with the shipload of valuable furs that he got in trade with the Indians. They began to realize that this new land might contain riches all its own.

Captain Samuel Argall soon followed Henry Hudson. In the summer of 1610, Argall's ship entered the Delaware Bay. He had been sent out by Virginia Colony at

Native Americans and Henry Hudson discuss a fur trade.

Jamestown to find food for the starving colonists. Captain Argall named the waterway in honor of Lord de la Warr, who was then the governor of Virginia Colony. The bay and the river soon became known as the Delaware. The Lenni-Lenape eventually became known as the Delaware Indians because it was often the custom of Europeans to name the native inhabitants after the area where they lived.

Other explorers came to the Delaware Bay. One was Cornelius Mey, a Dutchman who was thought to be the first European to actually land on Pennsylvania's soil. Cape May, New Jersey, is named after him. Another Dutch explorer, Cornelius Hendricksen, named the Schuylkill River in 1615. This river flows past Philadelphia and into the Delaware River.

As the Europeans became more prosperous, they were eager not only for such luxuries as spices, silks, and gems from the East Indies, but also for the furs that were plentiful in the New World. The Dutch realized that there was a fortune to be made in the fur trade. They built forts along the Delaware River to trade with the Lenni-Lenape. They traded tools, guns, cloth, and trinkets in exchange for furs. The Dutch did not try to settle this area because they were mainly interested in the fur trade.

New Sweden

The Swedes were the first Europeans who came for the specific purpose of settling. They set up a colony called New Sweden on the Delaware River in 1638, and they

Europeans trade tools for Lenni-Lenape furs.

began building log homes. The Swedes introduced the log cabin to America. Over the course of several more years, Swedish settlers arrived and the original Swedish colony moved farther up the Delaware River to Tinicum Island, which is a few miles south of present-day Philadelphia. The Swedes also established a thriving fur trade with the Indians.

It was not long before the area closest to the fort and settlements were **devoid** of animals. The Indians then moved inland to hunt and trap. The usually peaceful

Warring tribes battle in front of a U.S. fort. Many such clashes were the result of one tribe depleting its natural resources and attempting to take over a neighbor's territory.

Lenni-Lenape began to fight with the Susquehannock over their hunting grounds, and the Susquehannock in turn forced the Lenni-Lenape out of their traditional territory. The Lenni-Lenape fled into what is now Delaware or across the Delaware River into present-day New Jersey. The Lenni-Lenape were also forced to pay tribute to the Susquehannock. The Susquehannock in turn were at war with the Iroquois Nation, which lived in present-day New York.

Indian Wars

In the intense hunt for furs, the Iroquois began to hunt in the traditional territories of other tribes. The Iroquois

Nation was made up of five tribes: the Oneida, the Mohawk, the Onandoga, the Seneca, and the Cayuga. In the wars over furs, the Susquehannock sided with both the Erie and the Huron against the Iroquois.

The Indian Wars went on for a number of years. Many Native Americans were killed and the native tribes in Pennsylvania were reduced in numbers. The Iroquois Nation won this conflict and all the other Pennsylvania tribes came under its control. Many of the tribes such as the Erie and Shawnee were scattered and found new homes in what is now Ohio.

The diseases that Europeans brought with them also caused many Native Americans to die. The Indians had no **immunity** to smallpox and measles. Even a cold was deadly to the Indians. When William Penn arrived in his new colony, very few Native Americans lived in Pennsylvania. As more Europeans came to settle the new land, the Native American population was pushed farther to the West. The once powerful Susquehannock numbered only about three hundred warriors, and by 1700 the Delaware's population had shrunk to about four thousand.

The British

The Dutch eventually established settlements in present-day New York. The largest of these was New Amsterdam, which was situated where New York City is now. The Dutch also took control of New Sweden and the other Swedish settlements along the Delaware River. The Dutch in New Amsterdam governed them.

An artist's illustration shows an idealized picture of pioneer life in the Pennsylvania Colony.

Great Britain had established colonies all along the Atlantic coast, from present-day Georgia to New England. The only portion of the coast not under British control was the area that the Dutch controlled around New Amsterdam. On August 24, 1664, a British fleet of four ships sailed into the harbor and demanded that New Amsterdam surrender. The Dutch gave in quickly and did not resist. The Dutch flag was soon lowered and the British flag took its place. The Swedish settlements and the Dutch forts along the Delaware River and Bay were also part of this surrender; the inhabitants had to take an oath of **allegiance** to Britain. King Charles II of Great Britain gave this newly acquired land to his brother, James, the duke of York. The duke of York happened to be a good friend of William Penn. This eventually paved the way for William Penn's charter and the establishment of Pennsylvania Colony.

Chapter Three

William Penn's Holy Experiment

The founder of Pennsylvania Colony, William Penn, had many far-reaching ideas that were unusual for that day and age. He wanted to make his new colony a "holy experiment." He welcomed into his colony people of many different religions and backgrounds. Many of the beliefs that he expressed in his first constitution for Pennsylvania became part of the foundation for the United States of America. People came in large numbers to settle in a colony that offered them the freedom to worship as they chose without fear of **persecution**. This was a novel idea in the 1600s.

Establishing the Colony

William Penn's father was an admiral in the British navy. While Admiral Penn was in the service of King Charles II, the admiral had to pay—with his own money—for food to feed sailors on the king's ships. At the time of

Admiral Penn's death he had not been paid back for this debt. His son William asked the king for land in the New World instead of the actual money that the king owed to his father's estate. Because the king did not know the value of the lands in the New World, he was glad to give away land rather than money. Much of the duke of York's lands had been given to others to colonize, but the one large piece that remained was given to William Penn. In return William Penn paid the king a rent of two beaver skins each year and one-fifth of all the gold and silver found in the colony. This land stretched west from the Delaware River and contained about fifty thousand square miles. It also included the present-day

William Penn arrives in Pennsylvania in 1682.

state of Delaware. Penn wanted to call his colony New Wales or Sylvania, but the king insisted that it be named in honor of Penn's father, thus Pennsylvania was the name selected by the king.

Once the charter was established William Penn began to advertise his new colony throughout Britain and other parts of Europe. He wrote pamphlets encouraging people to come to this new land. One of his pamphlets read:

COME TO MY PROVINCE PENNSYLVANIA, WHERE YOU WILL FIND LAND YOU CAN OWN YOURSELF, PEACE, FREEDOM TO WORSHIP IN YOUR OWN WAY, AND A CHANCE TO TAKE PART IN GOVERNING YOURSELF.

Many people began to prepare for the long journey to this new colony and a new life.

The Colony Begins

In 1681, William Penn sent his cousin, William Markham, to Pennsylvania where he was to act as the deputy governor. Markham was to meet with the settlers who were living there and begin the process of setting up the government of Pennsylvania.

After much preparation and many delays, Penn finally arrived in his colony in 1682, aboard the ship *The Welcome*. He chose a site for his first settlement close to where the Schuylkill River meets the Delaware River. He called this new settlement Philadelphia, meaning the "city of broth-

Since the settlement of Pennsylvania Colony in 1682 the port of Philadelphia has grown and flourished, as seen in this nineteenth century engraving.

erly love" in Greek. He set about organizing a government for the colony. Before he left England he had written a document called *First Frame of Government*. This document was unusual because it stated that the colonists would have some control in how they would be governed. The document guaranteed a trial by jury, purposed an elected assembly to make laws, and allowed all males who owned property to vote. With this document Penn gave up some of his power as proprietor of the colony. As his colony grew, Penn revised the document twice and gave away even more of his power.

Thousands of people came to settle in Penn's colony. They were attracted by his ideas and the freedoms he proposed. They came so fast that it was impossible to

Amish families moved from Germany and settled in the Pennsylvania Colony.

build homes quickly enough. Many families had to live for a time in caves dug into the riverbanks. In 1682, about five hundred settlers lived in the colony. By the early 1700s, more than twenty thousand people settled.

The Quakers were the first large group to arrive. They were quickly followed by another large group of settlers from Germany, including the Amish and the Mennonites. They believed in humility, family, community, and separation from the rest of the world. A large number of them eventually settled in present-day York and Lancaster Counties. They were also called "Deutsch," which means German. They became what we know today as the Pennsylvania Dutch. The Scots-Irish were another large group of Protestant settlers that came from Ireland. They preferred to settle the frontier of Pennsylvania and moved into the western part of the state. The Moravians were yet another group who came to settle. Originally from Moravia in the present-day Czech Republic, they founded Bethlehem, Pennsylvania, and acted as missionaries to the Native Americans. William Penn's unique "holy experiment" was successful. It attracted people from many cultures and backgrounds who lived together in peace.

The Colony Prospers

Philadelphia soon became the largest city in the North American colonies. It attracted such men as Benjamin Franklin, who arrived from Boston as a young man in 1723.

Pennsylvania Colony became a prosperous settlement as more people arrived from Europe.

William Penn enjoyed life in his new colony. He built a beautiful home, called Pennsbury Manor, about twenty miles north of Philadelphia. He also visited the local Lenni-Lenape and learned to speak their language. He treated them with respect and kindness. William Penn made a number of treaties with the Indians. These treaties promised to pay them for their land and to give them the protection of the laws of the colony. The treaties lasted for seventy years. Penn's time in his new colony came to a close in 1684, when he returned to England to settle a dispute with Lord Baltimore over the boundaries for Pennsylvania Colony. William Penn did not return to Pennsylvania until 1699. This visit was short because political events in England again made it necessary that he return there in 1701. He never saw his beloved colony again; he died in England in 1718.

Many of the ideas that William Penn put forth in his *First Frame of Government* can be found in the U.S. Constitution. He not only founded a colony; but his ideas helped to found a nation.

Chapter Four

A New State in a New Nation

P ennsylvania Colony grew and prospered in the early 1700s. More settlements were established as the settlers moved westward. After William Penn's death in 1718, Penn's second wife, Hannah Callowhill Penn, and her children administered the colony. In fact, William Penn's descendants owned Pennsylvania until 1776, at which time the Pennsylvania Assembly ended the family's ownership. This assembly was originally founded by William Penn in his *First Frame of Government*. Over the years the assembly had become less and less dependent on the guidance of the Penn family. Once independence was declared, the ownership of all the former colonies ended. Pennsylvania, founded on the Quaker principles of tolerance and nonviolence, would soon be pulled into a serious and bitter conflict. This conflict would lead to a string of events that would cause some important changes for the colony.

A French general leads his troops and colonial allies against the British.

War Comes to Pennsylvania

The French and Indian War started in 1754, although it was not officially declared until 1756. This struggle, between France and Great Britain for control of North America, lasted for nine years. As Pennsylvania became more populated, land-hungry settlers began to move farther to the West. The French government, concerned about these new settlements on land that they claimed, built forts along Lake Erie and in the Ohio River valley to protect those claims. The forts allowed the French to control the entire Ohio valley until 1758. The French allied themselves with the Huron Indian tribe. These Native Americans raided the British settlements along the Pennsylvania frontier. It was a time of great unrest.

The French eventually lost the war to superior British forces and were forced to give up all their claims to land in Pennsylvania. Their former Native American allies continued to raid the settlements for a while after the war ended. Finally in 1763, the Indians were defeated at a place called Bushy Run and the Indian threat to the frontier settlements in Pennsylvania was over.

The British took over many of the former French forts. The fort that the French had called Fort Duquesne was rebuilt. It was renamed Fort Pitt. This fort is situated where the Allegheny and Monongahela Rivers come

The Huron, allies of the French, attack a British stronghold.

A bronze plaque depicts Benjamin Franklin, John Adams, and John Jay waiting to sign the Treaty of Paris that ended the French and Indian War.

together to form the Ohio River. It is the site of present-day Pittsburgh. The influence of the French faded from Pennsylvania and Britain was in control of all the colonies from Georgia to New England.

Taxes, Taxes, Taxes

Once the French and Indian War was settled and the Treaty of Paris was signed in 1763, the British were faced with debt **incurred** fighting the war. The British Parliament decided that because they had rid the colonies of the French, the colonies should help pay this debt. They began to **impose** a number of taxes on the colonies. The colonists resented these taxes because they had to pay taxes to England, yet they had no power in forming laws or controlling government. The British Parliament rejected these ideas and continued to impose unpopular taxes. When the colonists objected to one tax, it was **rescinded** but another tax was soon **levied** in its place. At different times there were taxes on stamps, paper, tea, and even powder for paint colors.

As the unrest in the thirteen colonies grew, delegates from each of the colonies except Georgia met in Philadelphia to address their concerns. This was called the First Continental Congress. The delegates met in September 1774. At that time there was not much talk of

The First Continental Congress met in Philadelphia to discuss Britains power over the colonists.

The Declaration of Independence was signed on July 4, 1776.

independence from Great Britain. They simply wanted to express their grievances to King George III. The delegates decided to meet again in May 1775.

There had been fighting in Massachusetts in the towns of Lexington and Concord between the British and the colonists. The unrest in the colonies was worsening. When the Second Continental Congress met in Philadelphia in May 1775, George Washington was appointed commander of the colonial forces, who were in open rebellion against the British. The delegates in Philadelphia debated and finally endorsed the Declaration of Independence. This was done on July 4, 1776, and proclaimed throughout the colonies on July 8, 1776.

On July 15, 1776, delegates met and began writing the first constitution for the new commonwealth of Pennsylvania. It was based on many of the ideas first proposed by William Penn in his *First Frame of Government*. The new constitution was not popular with a large portion of the population because it established just one elected assembly rather than two and a supreme executive council rather than a governor. It was rewritten in 1790, and it is much like the constitution that governs Pennsylvania today.

The Revolutionary War in Pennsylvania

A number of important Revolutionary War battles were fought in Pennsylvania. The Continental Congress was meeting in Philadelphia, so it was important to defend and protect this place of government of the newly

The U.S. Constitution was written and the Declaration of Independence was first read at Independence Hall in Philadelphia.

independent states. The British considered Philadelphia an important prize.

In the summer of 1777, the British invaded Pennsylvania. They sailed up the Chesapeake Bay, prepared to meet the colonial army near Brandywine Creek. Unfortunately, General Washington's troops lost the Battle of Brandywine. The result of this battle and a few other smaller battles enabled the British to occupy Philadelphia that September. The colonial government had to flee to York, Pennsylvania.

While the congress met in York, it adopted the Articles of Confederation, which loosely bound the former colonies together. In 1777 George Washington and his army spent a cold and dismal winter in Valley Forge, Pennsylvania. The troops lived in huts and had very little food or clothing.

After they lost the Battle of Brandywine, Washington and his troops used these huts, at Valley Forge, as their winter headquarters in 1777.

During that awful winter several military experts came from Europe to drill the soldiers and teach them how to march and fight. When spring finally came, the army was well-trained.

Cornwallis Surrenders

Thanks to the efforts of Benjamin Franklin, who was working for the Americans' cause in Paris, the French came to the colonies' aid with ships, troops, and supplies. This changed the outcome of the war. The British were finally forced out of Philadelphia and the government returned to the city. Philadelphia remained the capital of the new country until 1800. The end of the war came when General Cornwallis surrendered his army to George Washington at Yorktown, Virginia, on October 17, 1781.

Once the war ended, delegates from the thirteen former colonies met again in Philadelphia. In 1787, after much debate and discussion, the delegates drew up a constitution for the new United States of America. Pennsylvania became the second state to **ratify**, or approve, the constitution.

Pennsylvania grew into an industrial state with a large coal and steel industry. The first ironworks opened in Chester County in 1718, and by 1760, Pennsylvania led the colonies in iron production. In 1794, Pennsylvania also built the first toll road. The road helped settlers and traders quickly reach the western part of the state.

Pennsylvania also remained an agricultural state. It has some of the richest farmland in the world.

Today, Philadelphia is a thriving metropolis.

Along with growing corn, apples, tobacco, and even mushrooms, many dairy farms dot the hillsides in central Pennsylvania.

Pennsylvanians can be proud of the part that Pennsylvania Colony played in the founding and development of the nation. It truly deserves to be called the "Birthplace of a Nation."

Facts About Pennsylvania

Population: 12,288,000

Population density: Tenth

Size: Thirty-third

Land Area: 44,820 square miles

State capital: Harrisburg

Nickname: The Keystone State (also know as "The Quaker State")

State motto: Virtue, Liberty, Independence

State bird: ruffed grouse

State tree: eastern hemlock

State flower: mountain laurel

State dog: Great Dane

State insect: firefly

State animal: whitetail deer

Commonwealth: Pennsylvania, along with Kentucky, Virginia, and Massachusetts, has the designation "commonwealth." It refers to the well being of the public. The words "state" and "commonwealth" can be used interchangeably.

Natural resources: lumber, petroleum, natural gas, anthracite coal, bituminous coal

Major cities: Philadelphia, Pittsburgh, Harrisburg, Erie, Allentown

Major rivers: Delaware, Susquehanna, Juniata, Ohio, Allegheny, Monongahela, and Schuylkill

Ports: Philadelphia and Erie

Highest elevation: Mount Davis—3,213 feet

Mason-Dixon Line: Surveyed in 1763 to determine the border between Pennsylvania and Maryland. Often cited as the boundary between the North and the South.

Places to Visit in Pennsylvania

Philadelphia: Independence Hall, The Liberty Bell, The Betsy Ross House, Elfreth's Alley, Carpenter's Hall, Christ's Church, Benjamin Franklin's grave, City Tavern, Philadelphia Museum of Art

Bucks County: Pennsbury Manor, Bowman's Hill, Moravian Tile Works, New Hope

Harrisburg: Capitol Building

Valley Forge: Valley Forge National Historic Park

Chadds Ford: Brandywine Battlefield

Gettysburg: Gettysburg Battlefield

Lancaster County: Amish farms and communities, Landis Valley Farm Museum

Pittsburgh: Fort Pitt, The Nationality Rooms in the Cathedral of Learning at the University of Pittsburgh, The Carnegie Museum, The John Heinz Museum, Mount Washington Inclines, Point State Park

Erie: Presque Isle State Park, The Admiral Perry Monument

Wellsboro: The Grand Canyon of Pennsylvania

Glossary

allegiance: The fidelity owed by a citizen to a government.

declare: To state or assert.

devoid: Vacant, empty.

finance: To fund.

immunity: Protection against a particular disease.

impose: To apply or levy by authority.

incurred: Liable for.

levied: Taxed as a way to raise funds.

matriarchal: A society in which the mother is the head of her family group.

persecution: Suffering caused because of a belief.

provisions: Necessary supplies.

ratify: To approve.

rescinded: Cancelled or repealed.

For Further Exploration

Books

Isaac Asimov, *Henry Hudson: Arctic Explorer and North American Adventurer.* Milwaukee: Gareth Stevens Children's Books, 1991. This is the story of Henry Hudson based on what is known about his life and his voyages of exploration.

Jean Fritz, *What's the Big Idea, Ben Franklin?* New York: Coward McCann, 1976. Jean Fritz tells the story of Benjamin Franklin in an engaging manner. Franklin comes alive in the pages of this book.

Ruth Harley, *Henry Hudson.* Mahwah, NJ: Troll Associates, 1979. This is an easy-to-read book about the life of Henry Hudson and his search for the Northwest Passage to the Orient.

Arthur M. Schlesinger Jr., *William Penn: Founder of Democracy.* Philadelphia: Chelsea House, 2000. The story of the life and times of William Penn is told in an absorbing fashion. The reader learns of all the trials and triumphs that William Penn encountered as he founded his colony.

R. Conrad Stein, *Benjamin Franklin: Inventor, Statesman, and Patriot.* Chicago: Rand McNally, 1972. With a fresh insight, the many talents of Benjamin Franklin are highlighted in this book.

Paul A.W. Wallace, *Indians in Pennsylvania*. Harrisburg: Commonwealth of Pennsylvania, 1986. The culture of the Lenni-Lenape is presented in depth. The Susquehannock and other tribes that lived in Pennsylvania are dealt with in a much briefer manner. This book contains a great deal of useful information.

Charles A. Wills, *A Historical Album of Pennsylvania*. Brookfield, CT: Millbrook Press, 19996. This book offers interesting information about both the early history of Pennsylvania and its later growth as an industrial state.

Websites

How Did the Mason-Dixon Line Get Its Name? (www.ask.yahoo.com/ask/2000829.html). This website, presented in the form of a letter, gives the history of the 244-mile line that divides Pennsylvania from Maryland and was completed in 1767.

The Philadelphia Printshop (www.philaprintshop. com). This well organized website is easy to read. It details the history of the conflict and has a link to contemporary maps of the Revolutionary war.

Videos

Indians of North America: The Lenape. Bala Cynwyd, PA: InVision Communications, 1995. Members of the present-day Lenni-Lenape tribe discuss their culture and their history. It shows how they lived long ago and how they are keeping their culture alive today.

Battle of Brandywine: A Battle Lost—A Revolution Sustained. Harrisburg: Commonwealth of Pennsylvania, 1998. A filmed reenactment of the Battle of Brandywine. It explains how the American forces lost the battle and the consequences that followed that defeat.

Index